GAMES: A GATHERING AND GIFTING GUIDE
Collecting For Yourself And Others

Introduction

This is for folks who are just getting into the retro craze, or know someone who is *(like say your nephew who's having a birthday soon)*, or perhaps is just a skinflint and wants to wait until video games aren't $50 a pop before they buy them.

Contents

Section 1 What Are Your Needs?

Well… what ARE they? WHY do you want to collect old video games? Do you want a collection to impress your friends or fellow collectors? Are you looking just for what you want, with no regard for others? Is this a nostalgia tour? Are you looking on behalf of someone else? Depending on which of these it is, your ideal approach to buying a game would be radically different.

IMPRESSED FRIENDS?

If you want a collection to impress your friends, you'll need an idea of the kinds of games they like, what they'd consider noteworthy to possess. You could easily stock up on old sports games for example, those often aren't more than $5, depending on the system you could get 5 for that much, create an impressive collection of a hundred games for little more than $600, but if your friends wouldn't be into that then there's no point. Same with having every game for a system to impress a friend. The Wii is one of the best systems to pick on for this- a lot of vapid games were produced for it. Poorly done, may just be cashing in on a famous label. The Wii also has many fitness games to choose from, some aimed at individuals and some aimed at a whole family, hardly something a single individual would care to have in their collection, and if you're a fitness buff anyway you would likely get a bigger rush out of jogging around your neighborhood than jogging in place in your apartment, leaving your neighbors under you to wonder what the heck is going on. And of course we have the party games. You hardly need "101-in-1 Party Games" and "101-in-1 Sports Party Games", you'd spend much of the party trying to figure out what to play! Often such games end up being used rarely *(seriously, how many of us have a party often enough to justify having this, let alone parties where there'd even be an occasion to pull out a Wii?)*, and just collecting dust. I know firsthand because I've seen such games lying around people's houses, unplayed, and have been tasked with selling them.

FOR PARTIES

However, this goes towards intent. Is your intent simply to have a cheap party enhancer around? Then perhaps this is exactly what you need. Wiis sell for fairly cheap these days, around $50 as of this writing for one of the red models, so for perhaps $70 you could walk out of the game store with everything you need, games included. Wiis are also better for such a thing because of their affordability compared to the consoles *(for my purposes, "consoles" is a synonym for "systems", and it's a catch-all for any devices that are designed primarily to play video games, handheld devices included)* it competed against, PlayStation 3 and Xbox 360, which often sell for much higher prices and don't feature as many party game options.

COLLECTING TO IMPRESS COLLECTORS

Condition is most important for impressing collectors- brand new, mint condition, never used, and be sure it stays that way! This will be expensive. If what you're looking at isn't in the triple digits price-wise, it's probably won't impress a collector *(unless the person selling it is a total idiot or does not care; I once bought a $50 game at a pawn shop for $2.50, I met someone who found a $40 game at a yard sale for $5- but be careful! It might also be a fake)*. You will want to look at what the rarest video games are. Don't let the type of game fool you either, to be considered rare and expensive it doesn't have to be anything special, or really anything that someone in their right minds would pay such a price for. I own a $200 generic bowling game on the Nintendo 64, there is nothing special to it except that not so many of them were produced. It's not themed after anything, it's not Mario

Bowling or Donkey Kong Bowling or something, it's not the best bowling simulator that could ever be bought, it's just a game that they didn't make many of. The friend I got it from originally bought it from the store's discount section, such was the lack of regard it was treated with when it came out.

THE COMPLETIONIST

I mentioned completionist collecting- it sounds self-evident what to do, right? Buy every game there ever was. Well, are you SURE you want all of them? Is there a particular system that you're interested in? Does it matter if the games come with everything they would've had if you had bought them brand new? Even if you intend to own everything, there is still the question of where to start and how to proceed. Do you want to just buy them all willy-nilly, or have some pattern? Start with all the games you might actually play? Start with all the games from one publisher? Start with all of the games from a console family, such as perhaps buying every game on the PlayStations that were released? And what about imports, do you want to have any in your collection or do you just want all games released in your country? Maybe you want to start with a small system with a tiny library, so that within a smaller amount of time and at less expense you can claim to have completed collecting for an entire system? And what about video game accessories? Do you want every controller too? Every official accessory from light gun to power supply *(think NES Satellite for this one)*? You see, there are plenty of questions you need to ask yourself before starting down the completionist path. The simple directive of "buying it all" isn't so simple.

FOR YOU

Have you ever played a game before *(this is a legitimate question, it's entirely possible someone reading this might just be starting)*? Given all the types of games, you might very well have no clue what you're getting into. First, try to research the game. I don't mean read reviews, I mean look at pictures from it and watch a video of someone playing it. Unlike in times of yore, the internet these days makes figuring out what you want to buy a lot simpler, it's no longer sight unseen for the most part. Second, I'd suggest renting some games or borrowing them from a friend, just to get a feel for them. Watching a game in a video online and playing it are very different experiences. It might look perfect, gorgeous, and like something you'd enjoy playing, but then when it comes time to handle it you might find the visuals don't look good on your TV and the controls are terrible, and that the type of game itself isn't as fun as it looked. To get an idea of what games of a certain type you like and if you can't borrow or rent one, I'd suggest buying a cheaper console and some sample games, or perhaps some demo discs *(for those who don't know- demo discs came out for Sega Saturn, PlayStation/PS One, Xbox, GameCube, and Dreamcast- they contain demos of upcoming games, and most I've seen were $2-$15. Each disc usually has demos for multiple games, their purpose was to allow players to see demonstrations of upcoming titles, and they allow players to get a feel for how the featured games play)*. For you newbies keep in mind that just because you don't like one game from a certain style of games, it doesn't mean all games like that are bad. As an example for first person shooter games *(that is called a "genre", pretty much means category based on playing style)*, I do alright playing "Halo" but can't even get past one level in its contemporary "Medal Of Honor: Rising Sun". Even the same game can be totally different depending on what system you play it on- try Ultimate Mortal Kombat 3 on the Sega Genesis with its native 3-button controller versus on the SNES with its native 6-button controller; the difference in graphics and sound between contemporary consoles is already enough to alter the playing experience.

FOR NOSTALGIA

If you're having trouble remembering what games you had as a kid, try looking at pictures of your birthdays, or any pictures you have from around that time frame. Ask your parents; maybe they kept receipts. Search the internet as best as you can, which works for if you're trying to remember a game a friend had but are no longer in touch with that friend. If you know what systems you were playing, maybe looking at a list of games or a list of popular games would help. Once you do figure out what you want and buy it for the nostalgia value, something to try if you feel you still want to expand the selection is buying similar games. To give an example- I liked "Mario Kart" on the SNES, and playing it now triggers a nice nostalgia trip. But there's a game that uses similar methods to generate 3D on the SNES and has some similar colors, "Pilotwings", so because of how similar they look "Pilotwings" sort of triggers the same feeling. Unfortunately I can't tell you exactly how to find similar games in that sense, I don't know what triggers your nostalgia and the internet might not be much help depending on what the trigger is.

FOR SOMEONE ELSE

Get an idea of what they like to play, look at their game collection, and look at reviews of the game you intend to buy. As an example- just because someone likes James Bond movies, it doesn't mean they'll like a James Bond video game, and that series of video game adaptations is mostly done well! Some video game adaptations of movies, books, or TV shows are atrocious, or play nothing like what a fan of such a thing would be interested in. Of course it always helps to get a wish list out of the person. Another thing to watch out for is to make sure they don't have that game yet, haven't pre-ordered it, won't buy it before you have a chance to give it to them, or won't be getting it from someone else. And if you go into a popular store chain *(not going to name names but if you look at "Google Maps" and type in "video games" you'll see them, they're the stores that if you type the name in around a major city you'll see something like five or more of them)* keep in mind that the staff might try to push a particular product on you. I'd suggest going into a used game store that sells older video games systems, like GameCube/PlayStation 2/2001 Xbox or older. These stores normally sell recent games too, and the staff is often very helpful about what you should be looking for, but without an agenda to sell you something that might not be suitable. I've even overheard some direct their potential customers to another store if the customer wanted something that they didn't have, or was too new. This has been my experience, take it for the anecdote it is.

If your goal is not one I addressed above, I might not have needed to mention it yet but may address it later, so don't feel disappointed about the money you spent!

DO I NEED THAT VIDEO GAME SYSTEM?
Whether or not a certain video game console is needed for your collection is a good question. If you want to collect everything, then by all means buy it. But if you're collecting just to play the games, you might be able to save some money here. Some games can be played on other systems. PlayStation games *(PS One, the first PlayStation released, which is also just called "PlayStation")* for example can be played on a PlayStation 2 and early models of the PlayStation 3. If you already have one of those, or if you plan to buy one of them, you can skip buying an original PlayStation. If you're buying a game for someone,

make sure you're buying for the right hardware. One more point- if you buy one a video game system that supposedly plays games from a certain console but it is not that system and not even made by that system's company *(just making something up, but let's say you buy a SystemX from Constantine Productions, and SystemX is supposed to be able to play NES games even though SystemX is clearly not made by Nintendo, but might be entirely legal to sell because the hardware and software is different enough that copyright laws and patents aren't violated)* then make sure you research what that system can and can't play. I bought such a system once, a console that plays NES games that is NOT made by Nintendo, and while it plays most NES games, there are some it won't play.

Section 2 How And Where To Buy

Now that you've figured out what games you're looking for, you need to know where to get them. And really WHAT to get. Let's start with the what. Research is key here. What should your game have to be complete?

I'll dedicate this section to the Philips CD-I. When I first started buying games for it, I had no idea at the variety of cases they came in. Some are in long, hard plastic cases with cardboard slipcovers. Others are in CD cases with cardboard slipcovers. Some games like Tetris were released in both packaging styles. Overseas, the games were just released in a CD case, no covers. I did not know ANY of this, so I didn't know that some games and movies I had bought were missing slipcovers, and usually you won't find those items separately, so I unless I wanted two copies I was stuck with what I had bought. Then we get to the system itself- for you accessory collectors, make sure you know how things are supposed to be plugged in. The CD-I accepts wired video game controllers, but you plug the Player 1 controller into the back of the system. I didn't know this at first, so I thought the controller I'd paid $60 for was broken. Information about the CD-I was so hard to find that it was hours before I learned what I was doing wrong.

The CD-I is a good segue into something else to keep in mind- if your system can play video games from different countries, and your collecting-style permits it, it might be more affordable to buy games from another country. The CD-I lets you play games from anywhere in the world, so when I bought "Hotel Mario" and my CD-I controller, both came from the Netherlands. "Hotel Mario" was still the English release, it was a generic European version, and it was half the price that the American release of "Hotel Mario" would've been. Another example is "Mega Man 8" on the Sega Saturn. The Sega Saturn needs a special device that's maybe about $20 in order to play imported games, but the price difference is staggering with some of them. For a Japanese version, "Mega Man 8" *("Rockman 8" over there, another thing to research if you plan to buy an imported game is the game's name in that country.)* on the Sega Saturn is about $50. If I bought the English version on the Saturn, we're looking at $120. The only difference is that the dialog is in Japanese, but some games like that are so simple that you don't really need to read anything to enjoy it. In the case of "Mega Man 8", it's English version on the PlayStation is only $20 anyway, so if you wanted all the English dialog you could just buy that copy, or buy one of the compilations of Mega Man games released on later consoles *(PlayStation 2, GameCube, Xbox, Xbox One, PlayStation 4, Nintendo Switch).*

Just like with the CD-I, research what is supposed to come with a video game, and DON'T believe it when the seller says it's complete! Recently, I tried to buy a complete version of "Madden '96" on the SNES. It is supposed to come with the game, a cardboard backing for the game, a flyer advertising other Nintendo items, an instruction manual, a manual with safety information about the SNES, two charts that show the stats of the various football teams as they were that year, and the game's box which contains all of this in a nice package a little wider than a VHS. But when I went on eBay, I was seeing sellers listing the game as "new" and "complete" when it only featured the box, the manual, the cardboard, and the game. I had that same experience with "NFL Quarterback Club '96". It was supposed to have everything that "Madden '96" had, except instead of the team stat charts it had a green poster of some kind *(I still haven't bought it as of this writing so I don't know what's on the poster; I assume quarterback stats)*. However, just like "Madden '96", you'll see "complete" or "new" postings, or postings with some variation of that like "MIB" *(mint in box)*, but the item for sale is clearly missing the green poster. So make sure you know what's supposed to be there, don't just assume that if it's listed as "new" it has everything!

Speaking of physical aspects to research, make sure the game you are buying isn't a pirate copy or a reproduction. Legally-speaking, I have no idea what the difference is. Ethically speaking, pirates are trying to pass their copy off as the original while the reproduction ones are supposed to be openly copies of the original. Sometimes some fall through the cracks. I was on eBay trying to buy a copy of "Doom II" on the Game Boy Advance. I saw that they were usually going for $40, but then found one for $15. And then another. Finally I saw one of the lower-priced ones was described as a "reproduction". If you look at the picture though: virtually indistinguishable from the real version. I saw only a slight difference in shading on the label, that was it. But what made me suspicious was the price difference- sometimes you will see someone selling a game for $40 when it should be $15, but if you see a lot of games at $40 and only a handful at $15 *(and the games are all in the same condition, ie if the $40 are clean and in a box then the $15 are also clean and in a box)*, then something might be wrong.

Get an idea on what a fair price for the item you want is. If you plan to buy it at a store, try to know beforehand what a good price is. Some stores won't let you look up such information on your phone; I went to one where they throw you out if you do that *(that chain is no longer in business)*. It also makes for a faster shopping experience if you can gauge how reasonable the price is without researching it. This also should be done when buying online. Shop around. eBay often has the lowest prices, but not always. Watch out for bidding wars on eBay too, that item which started off as affordable might end up being way too expensive if you keep trying to outbid someone *(at this point it's natural for competitiveness to takeover, try to fight it)*. Amazon offers used items, and a surprisingly wide variety of old video games, so that's another place to go. Rarely, but occasionally enough that it's worth checking, a seller on Amazon might beat a seller on eBay. Don't put all of your eggs in the online basket though, going to the right store means that even accounting for gas mileage you'll get the best deal on that game.

Now that you know what possible compatibility issues there are, what a complete game looks like, and what a fair price is, it's time to buy it. You could make the assumption that what you see online is the best price; buy it there and move on. Nothing wrong there. You could also try browsing any yard sales in your area. You never know what someone will get rid of for a cheap price. I bought a $15 computer game at a friend's yard sale for a few quarters. I explained the pricing issue to him, but he was dismissive of it, so no I was not taking advantage of him or anything. Like I said earlier- some people just don't care. Local used video game shops are another avenue to pursue. What I mean by this are stores that aren't part of a big chain, maybe it's just a small business with only four stores in existence, or maybe it's just the one store and no others anywhere. Normally they sell any video game that comes into the store, whether from an Atari 2600 or a PlayStation 4. They're easy to find, usually I check "Google Maps" with a search that looks something like "video games". If you want to remove a hypothetical StoreX from your search because they're one of the big chains I mentioned that you know has terrible values, then on the map type "video games -StoreX" and remove some of the clutter. Contributing to these stores helps your local economy even more than the big stores, because the money doesn't go partly to some corporate office a thousand miles away to be spent in that thousand mile away region. Having this local shop in business also means other people looking to sell their potentially rare items might avoid the eBay bidding war and turn it over right there, allowing you to buy the item for less than what a bidding war would eventually yield, or even less than what the "buy it now" options allow for. If you know of some local shops but don't want to drive, just give them a call and ask what they have, if you know specifically what you are looking for. These small used video game stores also have a greater variety than the big chain stores by their very nature- accepting any video game from any era, so even if they don't have what you came in wanting you might come out with something you like. One drawback to the physical stores is that not all of them have their games arranged in alphabetical order, but don't feel self-conscious about asking the staff for assistance if you can't find what you want.

Pawn shops might be worthwhile too depending on what you are looking for. Mostly you will find consoles from the previous "generation". For those that don't know, a console "generation" is a group of competing video game systems with similar hardware and capabilities, Wikipedia outlines them pretty well. As of this writing, the current generation is Xbox One/PlayStation 4/Nintendo Switch, so while you would find those in pawn shops you would be more likely to find those from the last generation, Xbox 360/PlayStation 3/Wii. The ones from the last generation would also be at a cheaper price, and with cheaper games. Pawn shops have modernized a bit though and their video game pricing might be approaching what you'd expect from used games at a standard retail store, but there's still a chance to find good values. They also have some older systems, but when I went into one a month prior to this writing I noticed that it did not contain any video games or systems from before 2000.

PC Gamers have a problem here though- most small used video game stores and even pawn shops I've been in don't sell PC Games. Online shops might be your best bet there. Also make sure you have the right hardware- just because your PC can run something in a special compatibility mode doesn't mean that game will run. For those that don't know what I'm talking about, I'll use Windows as an example. It's an operating system for Microsoft computers. Operating systems are what let you use your machine, instead of having an expensive paperweight holding a bunch of inaccessible data. Windows has had different versions as the years have gone by. PC Games released for an early version of Windows might not work on a later version. Later versions of Windows allow you to run a program in something called "compatibility mode", where you can tell the computer that a program was made for an earlier version of Windows so it should be ran that way. This works with varying success. I've read online that it does, but in my personal experience I've found that it only works half the time. I mean with the same video game on the same computer, running it with the same compatibility settings, sometimes the game works and sometimes it doesn't. My point with all of this is to understand what operating system the game you want was designed for, and if possible use that operating system for that game, or at least the operating system which immediately followed it. That might mean buying an older computer, which I had to do.

Import games deserve a special section. For most video game consoles, you can't order a game from another region. If the game says NTSC-J, that means it won't run on an American system which is NTSC-US. Cartridge-based consoles often employed a simple mechanism for this- the cartridges in one reason were built differently from those in another, so it was physically impossible to insert it into the wrong system. As an added layer they have coding that checks what region the console is in. There are devices for bypassing all of that. Don't waste your money though on special microchips that supposedly bypass such lockouts, whether on discs or cartridges. Those are expensive, hard to install, and might not beat all of the protections anyway. I spent money on a PlayStation that had such a chip installed. It worked for some games and would allow me to play pirated games if I were inclined, but it did not work on all imported games. I had to buy the original hardware. When doing that, make sure you understand how to get that hardware to interface with your country's infrastructure. Each country has different electrical standards, that's why if you plug an American hair dryer into a European outlet without a converter it superheats. Look at what the electric standards are in the country you're buying from, and in your own country, and buy the necessary equipment. For my Japanese PlayStation I had to buy a small voltage converter box. You might need a special TV hookup too. That's not an issue from Japan to America, but from America to Europe it might be. U.S. and European TVs are in two different formats, NTSC and PAL.

Section 3 Cleaning And Testing

Before you leave the store, make sure a game is in the case or box you are purchasing. Normally discs are kept behind the cash register, out of their cases, and are only placed in the case upon purchase. Don't wait until you get home to find out they forgot something! When you do get home, test the game immediately *(if the store has a return policy, some don't so ask to test in the store in that case, but if you can take it home and test it do that so you're not "that guy" holding everyone else up. Do this for systems too, though these more often have a warranty.)*! Do this for any systems you buy too. Almost immediately. Clean it first. If the store has a disc cleaner, they'll look at your disc right in the store and clean it up if it is messy. Otherwise, you're on your own. For cleaning cartridges all you need is some rubbing alcohol and cotton swabs, and a cotton ball and rubbing alcohol for discs. Just because a store is selling it, even if they claim to have tested it, doesn't mean that what you're getting will work, or will work as advertised.

Sometimes when they test a game, they might just see if it powers on. Or they might not test it at all, or instead test a couple of the games some seller handed them and assume all worked. Sometimes games even come with errors that were probably there when brand new, and that no staff member at a video game store could reasonably be expected to find- I had a copy of a game on a disc where, despite the disc being in perfect shape, the game just froze at one point a third of the way in. It worked fine on all points before and after *(the game saved your progress onto the system, so I was able to use my brother's copy to get past the trouble spot, the error never resolved itself)*.

Another reason to test your game is that you might not be getting the game you expected. The label could be wrong, someone could've made a pirated copy with a good label, or in the case of cartridges someone might have switched the casing around the circuit board. I once bought a copy of "Pokemon", the Red version. When I plugged it into my Game Boy, it turned out that despite what the casing around the circuit board said *(it appeared to be an official Nintendo cartridge)*, the game was the Yellow version. That store had a return policy, so I was able to get that remedied right quick. I had to go back out anyway- I bought a game from another store that day which was supposed to have four discs, but only had three.

If your game doesn't work immediately once you've cleaned it, there could be other factors involved. Your system might be finicky. This is especially common with the boxy first model of the American NES consoles- many need a part necessary for reading video games replaced: the pins which touch the cartridges you insert, so not all cartridges will be read. Usually it's cheaper just to sell the console and buy a new one or one of the off-brand systems, so you start getting surpluses of NES consoles that may or may not work but the store owner wouldn't know unless he tested many games on them. If you have a disc-based console, the laser that reads your discs could be failing if the disc is not being read properly. The laser might also simply need to be cleaned; there are special items you can buy for that. I'm assuming of course that you did a thorough check on compatibility issues before now, but that is something else to double-check if relevant. The contacts in the cartridge slot of your system might need cleaning too, especially if it stops working because a gunky video game was inserted into it.

If you're buying on behalf of someone else and can't test it yourself, I'm not sure what advice to give. Try to test the game when the recipient is not looking? Claim you rented it, or borrowed it from a friend? For testing in gift-giving situations where you don't have the proper hardware at your house, I would recommend testing it in the store.

<u>Section 4 Protecting And Storing Your Collection</u>

This section almost entirely excludes people buying games as a gift. However, if you're not comfortable buying a game as a gift, you might get an idea in here for a gift that would help someone with storing their games.

For all games that come in cardboard cases, buy a protector for that cardboard. It will wear down from repeated handling. eBay is a good place for these. For cartridges that are on their own, buy protectors or at least dust covers. If you have any discs lying out on their own, they scratch easy to try a 3-ring binder with plastic "pages" that contain discs, or outright buy a CD case.

As your collection grows, you'll start finding that the usual standbys of next to the TV or with the blu-rays won't cut it anymore. Piling them up in a corner is inefficient, and depending on how high the pile goes you might be damaging the ones on the bottom from all that weight. A nice new bookcase would be good. But some of us are on a budget or move around a lot. I went to a so-called "big box" store for what I needed. I bought one of those stands that you put over a toilet, the ones with legs that go down on either side which hold up a shelf almost as far off the ground as the bars in a closet you'd hang a jacket or dress or suit from. I also bought hang-down closet shelves, which you might hang from such a bar in your closet. These shelves fold up to a small size when not in use, and are very cheap. The whole combination of bathroom stand and closet shelves was much cheaper and less space-consuming than a bookcase. There are also cheap hard plastic shelving units, stackable, at these "big box" stores. You get four tabletops and 12 legs, at least in the set I bought. I don't think stores really carry them anymore, but there also used to be storage racks that stretch almost 5 and a half feet tall, originally made for DVDs but which could be used for any systems that have games which come in DVD-like cases. It's a good option for if you have limited floor space, along with really anything that allows you to stack your items tall without putting them on top of each other. For smaller items, like loose Game Boy games *(if you aren't a perfectionist who has them all in boxes)*, I use one of the very small plastic filing cabinets. The ones that are less than a foot tall and have four drawers.

I'd suggest arranging your games alphabetically, it makes it much easier to locate them. But if you're the type who wants to play with their collection, it can get pretty hard to keep them in order. This is particularly true if space is an issue, and the games you want to get at are stacked up behind other games stacked up behind others in the back of a cabinet that also has all of your systems. It's going to be hard to get them back in order after taking them out, and if you know these are games you want to play over and over you might just leave them out of order.

For the consoles, what you might do depends on how much space you have. If you have plenty then it's no problem to spread them across several rooms or put a bunch around your TV without worrying about the space taken up by the games. I don't have that option, I just have one TV and a small space to put everything. My consoles sit stacked on top of each other. Most consoles can't work like that, so mine are all unplugged. Their TV hookups and power cables are stored in a bag nearby. The consoles are in a cabinet under the TV. Since I can only play one at a time, I take out one at a time and hook it up. Usually I'll leave it hooked up when it's not in use, since just one isn't very intrusive. I keep all the controllers separate from the consoles too, sitting on top of one of the hard plastic stackable tables I mentioned. Plastic filing cabinets would be a good solution for them too. Plastic filing cabinets could work for some systems, but not all of them. I don't believe the 2001 Xbox would fit, and I know an Atari 5200 would not fit.

Now, if you plan to hook everything up at once or are getting a gift for someone so inclined, the first thing that comes to mind is getting a selector box. You plug multiple video cables into these boxes, and press a button or flip a switch to determine which video cable's signal reaches the TV. They produce such boxes for any of the three types of video cables you will find with a video game system- HDMI *(one trapezoidal metal connection at the end of a cord)*, Composite *(three plugs per cable- one red, one yellow, one white- it looks like 3 different cables glued together)*, and RF *(one metallic cylinder at the end of a cable, with a single thin metal spike in the middle of the inside of the cylinder)*. There might be an issue with video game systems from before 1985, those require special setups to work, because of the types of cables they were designed to work with. For example- I have an Atari 7800 *(it was designed before 1985, just released late)* and it produces a horrible signal unless I use a specific type of cable, an analog RF cable. Even though this looks just like the cables that come after it and connects the same, it handles the signal differently. In addition to the box to plug everything into, you'll want to buy quality surge protectors and cable labels, so that you or the person you're buying for can more easily figure out which cable goes where. As for what to put the consoles on: if there's enough room in front of the TV and the furniture is correct for it, a shoe rack would be fine. Small multi-level tables to the side of the TV could work too. Whatever the arrangement is, if there is enough space to hook everything up then likely you will be able to find furniture to make it work.

<u>Section 5 Tracking Your Collection</u>

Unless your gift is a spreadsheet or your services in inventorying someone's collection, this section might only apply to the collectors themselves. I use Microsoft Excel. I have one page, under each column is a console. The top row states whether I have the console or not, and if I do have it what type it is (for example- is it the early boxy American NES, or the curvy one released later). I list in the rows under that what accessories I have, and then I list the games. Each cell that the game is in answers what the title is, how many I have *(sometimes I accidentally buy duplicates)*, if it has a case, if it has a manual, and what extras are with it *(such as system instructions, advertisements, etc)*. This makes for an unevenly-spaced list though, as some systems have games with much longer titles, or games that came with many more extras, than other systems. For that reason, separate pages in one spreadsheet, with each page dedicated to a system, would be a good alternative. I would also suggest a column for indicating the status of the item. Has it broken? Is someone borrowing it? Was it missing last time you checked? I didn't leave a column to indicate that, so I just change the color of the font or the background of the cell to indicate the status. I don't know about iPhones, but I know that on Android or Blackberry phones doing a spreadsheet for the list makes it portable- just upload it onto your phone. I've been saved from buying duplicates of video games plenty of times by being able to reference my list while in a store.

Another type of spreadsheet you might consider doing is one of games you want. It would look similar to the one for games you have. As mentioned before, video games are supposed to have certain items with them if they're brand new, so it would be helpful to know what it is that's supposed to be there with it if you glimpse it in a store. I ran into that with a game that I bought at a store. I thought it was complete because the manual was in there and I assumed, wrongly, that someone wouldn't just throw out an extra but keep the manual. I didn't know until much later I was wrong, and now I need to look for a complete copy to find the needed extra. You could also add the common prices for games you want to this spreadsheet, which would make checking if the store is giving a fair price a very quick endeavor, as opposed to browsing eBay auctions on your phone while standing in the middle of an often-cramped store *(these non-chain used games stores are often very small, and the friendly staff might even be engaging you in conversation, so being able to check the price quickly helps)*.

<u>Section 6 Selling Your Collection</u>

It happens. My cousin loves collecting video games, but has had to sell all of his before because he needed the money. The same could happen to you too. Should such a dreaded day come, having your spreadsheet of what you have already will cut a lot of time. You would just need to add a price to everything. Having your games neat, organized, and stored properly helps here too. They won't be damaged form storage, and when it comes time to prepare them for sale they're easily found.

When you go to sell them online, make sure you understand what you're getting into. Craigslist I don't think takes a cut out of what you sell, but regardless of if you have to pay or not to post such an ad you are still putting yourself at risk, given the kinds of folks that stalk that site. eBay takes a cut of your sale, and has almost no buyer protection. I bet there's plenty of people on there ready to scam a first-time seller out of something. I cannot comment on Amazon; I have no experience with them. I would assume they're similar to eBay though.

Price your material fairly, set a baseline for what to expect, then try to get people to bid on what you sell. Even on Craigslist it's possible, though many on there expect garage-sale prices. This is why Craigslist and eBay might be more advantageous than Amazon, which has a price set in stone *(nothing wrong with that, it's a less risky method for both buyer and seller)*. Before setting your price, also make sure shipping is accounted for. This should either be in the price itself or as a separate statement. If the price already looks high, it might look better to list shipping separately.

<u>Section 7 Simple Section Summaries</u>

Section 1 What Are Your Needs?
        Ask yourself:
                -Why are you collecting?
                -What should you start your collection with?
                -Does condition or completion matter?

Section 2 How And Where To Buy
        -Research first: know what price to pay and what you should be getting
        -Find locations, online or in person.
                Try to find small Mom & Pop video game
                stores, their staff is usually very helpful

Section 3 Cleaning And Testing
        -rubbing alcohol, cotton balls for discs, and cotton swabs for cartridges and systems
        -test systems in the store if they don't have a warranty, test games at home only if the
         store has a return policy

Section 4 Storing Your Collection
        -bookcases, tables, shelves, shoe racks, DVD stands
        -protectors for any cardboard cases or loose discs and dust covers for loose cartridges

Section 5 Tracking Your Collection
        -spreadsheets containing systems, games, what came with them, condition, location

Section 6 Selling Your Collection
        -know what you have and its value
        -know the risks to you, and don't assume all buyers are nice people
        -know what policies the site you are selling on has
        -try to spark a bidding war